OVER RAINBOW BRIDGE

An ABC Dog Adventure

KAREN NICKSICH

CONTRIBUTOR ~ RACHEL NICKSICH

ILLUSTRATOR ~ HELEN

KAREN MARIE NICKSICH
Copyright © 2022

Story concept by Karen Marie Nicksich

Contribution by Rachel Nicksich

Original artwork by Helen - www.flowerpup.com

Flower artwork by pixabay.com

Book design by www.delaney-designs.com

ISBN 9781662932144 Hardcover

Dedication

To: Any child who has loved and lost a dog

Dogs are love in its purest form

Max

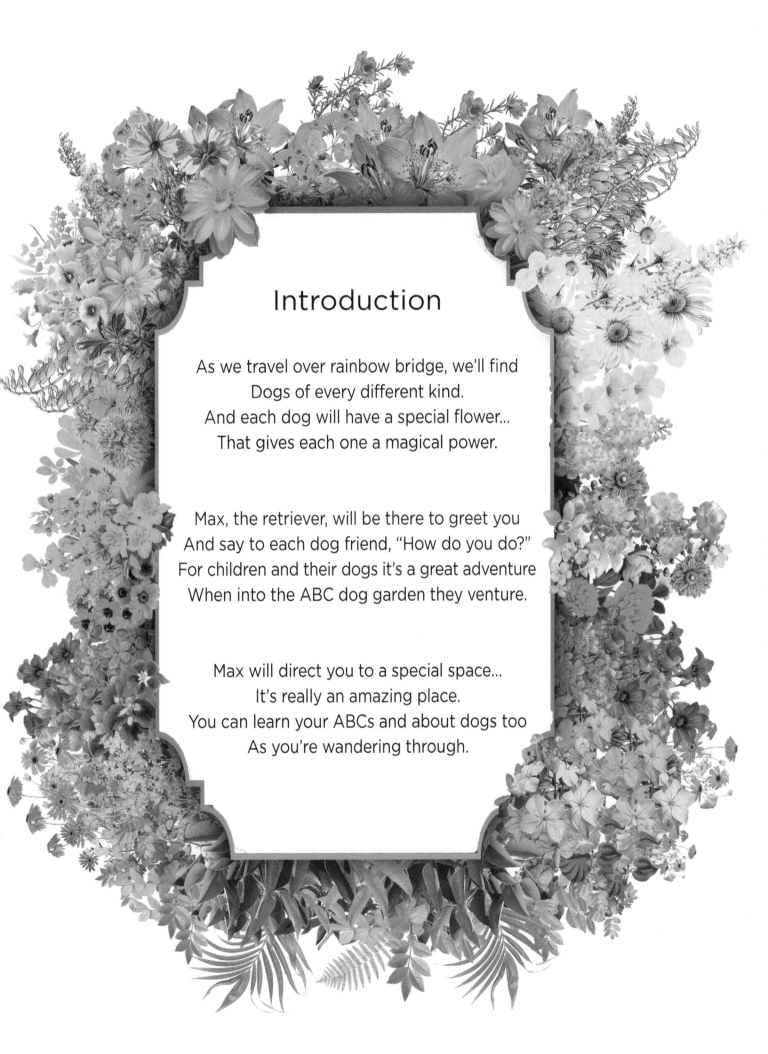

Introduction

As we travel over rainbow bridge, we'll find
Dogs of every different kind.
And each dog will have a special flower...
That gives each one a magical power.

Max, the retriever, will be there to greet you
And say to each dog friend, "How do you do?"
For children and their dogs it's a great adventure
When into the ABC dog garden they venture.

Max will direct you to a special space...
It's really an amazing place.
You can learn your ABCs and about dogs too
As you're wandering through.

A

is for Ajax the Akita.

He was first bred for hunting in Japan...

Making him part of your family would be a good plan.

He's admiring the Azaleas and he's bold.

He'll be affectionate and loyal as you both grow old.

Be **A**mazing

Ajax

B

is for Bella the Basset Hound.

She's happy as she bounces through the Beebalm...
Even though she's active, inside she's quite calm.
Her sensitive nose loves the scent of flowers.
She can wander in the garden for hours.

Be **B**old

Bella

is for Cho the cheerful Chinese Shar-Pei.

Even though he's quite wrinkled, he's not really sad...

Being camouflaged in the Chrysanthemums makes him feel glad.

As a watchdog, he'll guard you with his strong mind.

There's no better companion you could ever find.

Be Caring

Cho

D

is for Dante the Dalmatian.

He's filled with energy and loves to play.

He might wear you out by the end of the day.

No one could ever accuse him of being lazy

As he **d**ashes around smelling each **D**aisy.

Be Dedicated

Dante

is for Edward the English Bulldog.

He is **e**xcellent with children and a true friend.

He will defend you until the very end.

As the day draws to sunset's dramatic close

He **e**njoys the scent of the **E**vening Primrose.

Be Engaged

Edward

is for Felicity the Fox Terrier.

She is **f**ocused on being part of your family tree.

She's alert, lively, and smart as can be.

From the grass-like **F**oxtails she stays away

So there's no danger when she wants to play.

Be Fierce

Felicity

is for Gus the Great Dane.

He enjoys **g**lancing at the **G**ardenia in bloom.

He thinks the outdoors is one big garden room.

He was bred to gather game as a retriever

But today he's a furry people-pleaser.

Be Grateful

Gus

H

is for Helen the Husky.

She can **h**aul heavy loads of **H**ydrangea flowers...

Sled-pulling ability is one of her superpowers.

She can jump a fence that is more than **h**igh,

So treat her well so she doesn't try.

Be Honest

Helen

is for Izabella the Irish Setter.

With reddish-brown fur and a fun-loving heart,
She becomes part of your family at the very start.
As she interacts with children, she's intelligent and fair
And she loves the scent of the Iceland Poppies you share.

Be **I**nquisitive

Izabella

J

is for Jasper the joyful Jack Russell Terrier.

He's so very clever and so very cute...

He looks like he's wearing a brown and white suit.

He enjoys jumping and barking at squirrels in the park

And loves the smell of July's Jasmine after dark.

Be Joyful

Jasper

is for Kenneth the Keeshond.

With a furry coat of black, cream, and white,
He can stay warm on a cold winter's night.
Being a kind friend is one of his superpowers
And he enjoys Kangaroo Paw flowers.

Be **K**ind

Kenneth

L

is for Luna the Labrador Retriever.

In freshwater lakes, she loves to swim...

During the summer she can't wait to jump in.

She feels joyful and lighthearted you can tell

As she takes in the Lavender and Lilies of the Valley smell.

Be a **L**eader

Luna

M

is for Madison the Bernese Mountain dog.

She can do almost anything you ask

Because she knows how to multi-task.

She marvels at the Marigolds every day

As she takes time from work to play.

Be **M**agical

Madison

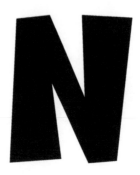

N

is for Nathaniel the Newfoundland.

A huge bear-like dog with a furry coat...

He was bred to pull a very large boat.

He navigates the neighborhood with ease

As he romps in the Narcissus with its long leaves.

Be **N**ice

Nathaniel

is for Oddie the Old English Sheepdog.

When you accompany him on his daily run,

He is outgoing and oodles of fun.

He's playful, but is really too big to hide

And he's overjoyed with the Orchids outside.

Be **O**pen-minded

Oddie

P

**is for Princess
the Standard Poodle.**

She is active, perky, and very polite

And her "hairstyle" is quite an appealing sight.

She's excited about the flowers she's found—

Lots of purple Petunias she parades around.

Be **P**atient

Helen

Princess

Q

is for Quincy the Queensland Heeler.

He looks like a fox with his sharp, pointy ears

But if you want him for a pet, you shouldn't have fears.

He's a great guard dog for your family's place

And he quickly searches for Queen Anne's Lace.

Be Qualified

Quincy

R

is for Ra'shawn the Rodesian Ridgeback dog.

He's intense, brave, and strong...

With him to protect you, you can't go wrong.

He's radiant as he views each Rose

And breathes in the beautiful scents through his nose.

Be **R**espectful

Ra'shawn

S

is for Sebastian the Shih Tzu.

He's **s**tubborn and **s**ensitive to both praise and blame...

When you give him a compliment, say his name.

He's a **s**imply **s**pectacular **s**ight

As he looks at **S**unflowers in the morning light.

Be **S**elf-confident

Sebastian

T

is for Teddy the Tiberian Mastiff.

With family he's friendly, but to others he seems rough.

His size is scary to strangers and he acts tough.

But he's a gentle giant in the garden, it's true—

Smelling the Tulips is fun for him to do.

Be **T**hankful

Teddy

is for Unity the Utonagan.

She looks like a wolf, but she isn't one.

Three breeds were mixed just for fun.

She is **u**nique and almost always **u**pbeat.

For her, seeing the **U**inta Cactus is a special treat.

Be **U**nderstanding

Unity

is for Vara the Vizsla.

If you want to go out for a jog,

She will absolutely love coming along.

At work and at play she is intensely glorious

And when she discovers **V**iolets, she's **v**ictorious.

Be a **V**isionary

Vara

is for Winnie the Wippit.

She's **w**arm-hearted, short, and has a cute foxy face,

And if you let her, she'll take over your place.

She lays a pile of **W**aterlilies at the feet

Of the Queen of **W**ales when they meet.

Be **W**himsical

Winnie

X

is for Xavier the Xoloitzcuintli
(pronounced *show-low-itz-QUEENT-lee*)

He is a hairless dog originally from Mexico.

He signs his letters with XOXO.

He doesn't think a more lovely flower could ever be

Than the extraordinary Xyris from the yellow grass family.

Be in Xanadu

Xavier

Y

is for Yasmin the Yorkshire Terrier.

She has a cute black button nose
And her long hair is tied up with bows.
"Yaba-daba-do" is what her barking yells
When she sees the Yellow Bells.

Be **Y**oung at heart

Yasmin

is for Zuri the Zuchon.

She fits in with a crowd of stuffed toys
And her fluffiness delights girls and boys.
Being around Zinnias makes her feel zen
She falls asleep again and again.
ZZZZZZZZ!

Be Zen

Zuri

THE END

Cooper

HOW TO HELP CHILDREN WHEN THEY LOSE A DOG

Saying good-bye to a pet is really hard. The best thing you can do to help your child cope with pet loss is communicate openly. Keep your explanations simple and in age-appropriate terms. Some children may think their pet died because of something they did; Make sure to offer reassurance that such is not the case.

- A special way of saying good-bye is called a "Memorial." This has the word memory inside it. Draw a picture of a favorite memory you had with your dog and share it with your family, teacher or counselor.

- What does Rainbow Bridge look like to you? What is your dog doing? Draw a picture and send it to me with just your first name and age.

- For older children, draw what grief looks like to you and talk to your parent how you feel.

- Plant a flower in memory of your dog.

- Write a letter to your dog when you are feeling better.

- What lesson did you learn from your dog? Write it down and send it to me.

- Finally, if this booked helped you tell your teacher or friend about it.

Karen Nicksich / emeraldhalo@earthlink.net

Karen and Maddie

About the Author

A nominee for Disney Teacher of the Year, **KAREN NICKSICH** was a teacher for 34 years in the BYU/Salt Lake City School District after earning her M.Ed. She also has certificates in gifted and talented education and in English as a Second Language.

Karen is very proud of teaching her students to write service learning grants. Her 4th grade class won the *State Farm Giving Back Service Award*. All her 4th grade students learned how to make and play Native American flutes, and presented a Native American play in which they played the flutes. They also raised money to provide water to Native Americans living in southern Utah. During summer vacations, she developed holistic crystal collars for dogs—chakra collars for well balanced dogs, grounding collars for aggressive dogs, and healing collars for dogs with disease.

After moving to Washington twelve years ago, Karen suffered a severe concussion and lost her ability to drive, type, remember recipes, and had no idea who people were. It was clear she could not continue teaching, so she began writing stories about dogs as a way to learn to type again.

She won the gold medal from the *Wishingshelf Award* in the UK, and the bronze medal for *Gus Finds His Way Home*. She won bronze medals from the *Healthy Living Award* for *Earth Angels*, a photo documentary of specially-abled children and the 2021 bronze medal for Everyone Needs a Little HOPE, the bronze medal for *Gus Makes a New Friend* from the *Illumination Awards*, and the *Pinnacle Award* for several of her other books.

www.pet-angelreader.com

Hi, my name is Rachel.

I am 31 years young. I grew up in Salt Lake City, Utah. Twelve years ago we moved to Richland, Washington. I live with my father, John, my mother, Karen and my brother, William. Our family has two dogs. Their names are Maddie and Gus. I enjoy baking, fishing and being an advocate for specially-abled children.

One of my favorite activities is making necklaces for people. I call them Penguin Pearl necklaces because I love penguins and cold water. In ten years, I look forward to having a family of own and traveling to different parts of the world.

Rachel

Hi, my name is Pamela.

I am a graphic designer with a passion for art. After years of working for newspapers and commercial printers, I decided to start my own business over 20 years ago. Delaney-Designs, a vision of your thoughts, is my motto.

I am blessed to have three grown children and three grandchildren.

Charlie is my sister's dog whom I would dogsit for often. Charlie was a gentle giant who has crossed over the Rainbow Bridge. This image brought sheer joy to me and my sister.

Diesel, my sister's newest addition, will mirror Charlie in many ways, such as, he will squeak a ball with his nose, just like Charlie. We all smile.

www.delaney-designs.com

Pamela and Charlie

My name is Helen (Elena).

I am an Italian mom who loves graphics design.

After a pet loss, my husband and I decided to find a way to help people cope with the bereavement... so i contacted freelance artists from all over the world who want to share the mission with me... this is why Flowerpup exists!

www.flowerpup.com.

Hi, my name is Veronica.

I was born in Salt Lake City, Utah and currently lives in a small community just outside of the city. I am married to the love of my life Lowell. I have one daughter Ashley, her sweetheart Michael and their three children Malachi, Irene, and Audrey who light up her life. Her husband brings five children to the marriage, Holly, Heather, Heidi, Hailey, and Travis with their husbands and wife eleven grandkids and two great grand kids. We are blessed.

I love to write for children and has written three books and created a matching card game set before creating the matching coloring book for this book.

She also enjoys fishing, camping, reading and spending time with friends and family.

www.infiniteheartseries.com.

Veronica Koplin

Hi, our names are Tiffany and the Page Girls.

Jali, Natalie, and Tiffany Page enjoyed illustrating this book and all three of them love reading. They hope that you enjoy it too! They love dogs, and have a Miniature Schnauzer, Joey, and enjoyed drawing all the dogs in this coloring book.

Their mom, Jali, is a very talented artist, she met her college sweetheart & married him. They had three children (two of them worked on the matching colorbook) and they have lots of unconditional love for them.

Tiffany is 10 years old; she loves reading, and if she finds any paper will quickly go through it.

Natalie is a very incredible artist and has a massive library, she is 13 years old.

The Page Girls love to call North Salt Lake their home.

Tiffany Page

Printed in the USA
CPSIA information can be obtained
at www.ICGtesting.com
LVHW061654221123
764421LV00013BB/1042